DARE TO *dream*
DARE TO *act*

UNLOCK YOUR IDEAS
TO GREATER SUCCESS

Jack

To a great

Iowa Promoter

17

DARE TO *dream*
DARE TO *act*

UNLOCK YOUR IDEAS
TO GREATER SUCCESS

BY TERRY RICH

WITH MARY GOTTSCHALK

Business Publications Corporation Inc.

Dare to Dream Dare to Act is published by
Business Publications Corporation Inc., an Iowa corporation.

ISBN-13: 978-1508702528
ISBN-10: 1508702527
Library of Congress Control Number: 2015905935
CreateSpace Independent Publishing Platform, North Charleston, SC

Business Publications Corporation Inc.
The Depot at Fourth
100 4th Street
Des Moines, Iowa 50309
(515) 288-3336

Table of Contents

Acknowledgments

Many say their #1 fear in life is speaking in front of people. That's the easiest thing for me to do ... I love to tell stories, to make people feel good by sharing bits and pieces of the story of an ornery kid who thought he had a better idea.

What's hard for me has been capturing the personal thoughts and ideas behind those bits and pieces. Even though I've lived the stories, getting them into the book that you're holding has become my most difficult adventure.

This project allowed me to appreciate:

- and respect the professional talents of editor and writer Mary Gottschalk. Her past business wisdom, combined with a strong writing background, helped weave my passions into lessons you might enjoy.
- the skills and professionalism of the staff of Business Publications Corporation (particularly Ashley Holter, and Brianna Schechinger) who took a fun read and made it even better.
- my wife, Kim, and family who let me dream while, at the same time, kept me humble.
- the "nomans" who told me why I couldn't do something but, in a way, inspired me to show I could get it done.
- wanting to be a better "encourager" of people, family and co-workers.

So here's to the next great idea.

– Terry Rich

Introduction

A lot of people view Terry Rich as a force of nature.

Is it because he's naturally creative or because he's managed to bring so many of his ideas to fruition, often against considerable odds? Is it because his "down-home farmer-friendly" personality can inspire and motivate others? Is it because he is always searching for a new and better solution to any challenge?

Terry would tell you that his success reflects a combination of old-fashioned gumption and a lot of lucky breaks. And that he's been determined since childhood to have fun along the way.

I would say that it's all of the above.

I first got to know Terry when I served as chair of the search committee to find a CEO for the Blank Park Zoo in Des Moines, Iowa.

At the time, the zoo was in a world of hurt. After two decades as a department of the city of Des Moines, the zoo had almost disappeared from the community's radar screen as an entertainment venue. Despite the recent opening of the $6.7 million Discovery Center and the addition of several other new animal exhibits, attendance was poor.

By 2002, the city was no longer willing to subsidize the recurrent operating losses of the zoo, and in 2003, it turned management of the zoo over to the Blank Park Zoo Foundation. While the zoo was now free to operate without bureaucratic constraints, the donor community was exhausted from the just-completed $8 million capital campaign. It was clear to the board of the foundation that the zoo would not long survive if it could not increase attendance and improve operating cash flow.

The board's dilemma was that most of the zoo's staff, all employees of the city, had long functioned in a politicized environment that abhorred risk-taking and favored long-established procedures and protocols. The foundation wanted a CEO with the imagination to engage the community and invigorate the staff.

The board wanted a flag carrier to lead the charge.

That description suited Terry to a T. From the first day I met him, he impressed me as one of the world's greatest promoters. I was struck by his spontaneous and creative response as I described the various challenges facing the zoo.

Hiring Terry was a turning point for the zoo, as his creative spirit and boundless enthusiasm were contagious. He was able to fashion good relationships with people, even as he challenged the old ways. One of his early successes was the transfer of staff from the municipal union to the zoo payroll, with 401(k) plans and bonuses based on performance. Some 90 percent of the staff elected to leave the union and accept a position at the zoo.

Terry challenged everything about the zoo's operations. By tradition, for example, zoos are free or charge very low admission fees. Not surprisingly, skeptics abounded when he decided to more than double the admission fee, on the theory that people would place more value on the zoo if the tickets cost more. But he didn't want to shut out those who might not be able to afford the new ticket price, so he arranged to distribute discount coupons and free passes to underprivileged groups.

As he predicted, attendance and revenues went up.

His most significant contribution, however, came from the programs that put the zoo "on the map"—activities and events that would have been unimaginable under the city's regime. One of the first was a radio broadcast of a parade in which various Des Moines celebrities led animals down the streets of the city. It was an April Fools' Day spoof, but it brought thousands to the zoo in the following months.

Another break with tradition was Zoo Brew, an after-hours, adults-only event that would, for the first time ever, serve beer and wine to visitors. Again, attendance went up. The first night, Zoo Brew drew only a few hundred people, but my understanding is that it now draws two to three thousand adults each week during the summer months.

A list of the innovative programs Terry and his staff brought to the zoo over the next few years would take more space than I have here. The proof of the success of his approach lies in the numbers. For the first full year of his tenure, attendance rose by some 30 percent, while the operating deficit was cut more than 50 percent. Attendance continued to increase, and by Terry's third year, the zoo was operating at a profit. In 2006, the Iowa Tourism Office noted that the zoo was the second most attended venue in the state of Iowa.

Terry had a powerful influence behind the scenes as well. At the time he joined the zoo, the foundation board was dispirited from years of trying to support an organization patently unable to accomplish its mission. Not long after he arrived, Terry reenergized the foundation when he organized a trip to Africa for board members and major donors.

That trip was one of the greatest experiences of my life. All of us came away from that very collegial experience with a much greater sense of the need for conservation as a general matter as well as through our own animal care practices. Board members came home with a much greater sensitivity to the needs and opportunities at the zoo; non-board members returned far more sensitive to the need for generous funding.

Throughout his time at the zoo, I felt that Terry had a clear sense of his own strengths and weaknesses. I was not surprised when, in 2009, he decided that he had done all he could do for the zoo. As much as I understood, I was sorry to see him leave.

There is no question that Terry accomplished exactly what the board asked him to do. He put pizazz into the zoo's image and laid a strong foundation for the zoo to build on.

Terry nailed it solidly.

Terry is a dreamer who dares to take action. My admiration for him is complete.

Bob Burnett
Retired President, CEO, Board Chair
of the Meredith Corporation

Chapter 1

A Fateful Cup of Coffee

It all started with a cup of coffee.

My hometown, Cooper, Iowa, was proud to be celebrating its centennial in midsummer 1981. Gerald Lawton, a local farmer in charge of publicity, wanted to invite the world, but except for a church ice cream social, he couldn't remember when Cooper had any publicity of any sort. Now, he needed help with press coverage for the event, a mere nine weeks away.

In its heyday, Cooper had a bank, a grocery store, a blacksmith shop, and all the conveniences for a comfortable life. On the day Lawton and I met for coffee, however, the church, the school, and a maintenance garage were all that was left standing—and the town had only fifty residents.

At the time, I was general manager for Heritage Communications, one of the area's pioneering cable companies. Lawton figured that if I could successfully market cable TV during the days when cable wasn't at all cool, I could drum up interest in the centennial.

"And," Lawton added, "you're the most famous person we've had from Cooper. You've even done TV commercials."

"Wow," I replied. "If I'm the most famous person in one hundred years, we'd better adopt someone."

An idea was born.

Over a bottomless cup of coffee, we decided to ask all fifty residents to write to their favorite celebrity, requesting him or her to apply to be the honorary fifty-first resident. Every resident would get one vote for the winner. We made up Iowa-sounding questions that applicants would have to answer in order to qualify:

Do you own a pair of bib overalls?

What's the difference between an apple pie and a cow pie?

Have you ever hunted snipe?

Have you milked a cow?

Have you chewed tobacco?

Isaac Cooper was the founder of Cooper. Who was buried in Isaac Cooper's grave?

Tongue-in-cheek questions, for sure. But we knew that busy celebrities would need an incentive to reply, so we came up with prizes for the winner:

Free burial plot at the cemetery of your choice (Cooper had four available, all with very scenic views).

A lifetime pass to the Cooper tennis court (the applicant may need to mow before playing).

Free lifetime fishing rights to Cooper's secret fishing hole.

A free oil and lube from the garage of your choice in Cooper.

One free week for your family at a real Iowa farm of your choice (meals, horseback riding, and farming chores included).

When I left the coffee shop an hour later, I thought the project sounded like fun. Then too, generating some decent media coverage would be a nice "give-back" to my community.

After composing a one-page press release, I headed for the library in search of information on news media. Finding only an ancient reference book, I addressed plain white envelopes to the ten key media outlets in Des Moines.

Somehow, I still had thirty-four envelopes left. "OK," I told myself, "let's have some fun."

I addressed the remaining envelopes to any media outlet that looked impressive, including the *New York Times*, the *Miami Herald*, ABC, and the *National Enquirer*. After forking out $42 in postage and printing, I managed to get the press releases in the mail by 5:00 p.m.

The first call came at 9:05 a.m. the next day.

"Hi, this is Bruce Kanner with United Press International. Tell me about Cooper. I'd like to put the story on the national wires." I was thrilled, but I wanted to be sure that whatever he did would play well in the local *Jefferson Bee and Herald*. National publicity wouldn't be so great if the townsfolk were portrayed as hicks.

Barely thirty minutes later, the phone rang again. "Hello, this is Jim McCawley. I'm a talent coordinator for Johnny Carson's *Tonight Show*. I saw the UPI wire story that landed on Johnny's desk, and as you know, Johnny was born in Corning, Iowa."

I assumed the call was a practical joke from a friend I'd told about the promotion. "Quit pulling my leg. We're trying to get some press here."

Cooper, Iowa

Dear

On JULY 11, 1981, the 50 residents of Cooper, Iowa will have its centennial and will choose one famous person to be its 51st resident. You see, Cooper is not very well known, which is fine, but we would like to have at least one resident who is famous to adopt for our centennial day.

The competition is stiff and we're getting a lot of entries, but we feel that you should be in on this contest. This is your exclusive entry form...

Please fill out the attached form and send it to:

    51st Star Over Cooper
    P.O. Box
    Cooper, IA   50059

Please do not delay. Entries are due July 1, 1981. You would not be expected to attend the centennial, but would receive the following if you were chosen:

1. One free burial plot in the cemetary of your choice (4 are available with very scenic views).

2. A lifetime tennis pass to the Cooper tennis court.

3. Free fishing rights to Cooper's secret fishing hole.

4. Free oil and lube from the garage of your choice in Cooper.

5. One free week for your family to a real Iowa farm of your choice - (all meals, horseback riding, and farming chores included).

As you can tell, we are proud of Cooper and hope you can help us by simply entering this contest for fun. If you have any questions, please call us at (515) 386-4585.

Sincerely,

Cooper Resident

Official Cooper nomination letter

"Don't hang up," the man pleaded. "I really am calling from LA! I'm going into a staff meeting to talk about the Cooper story. But I need your word that we'll be first to air it, no matter who else calls you."

"I guess we can give you first shot," I quipped. *Yeah right.* Why shouldn't we commit to Johnny Carson? It's not as if we were going to get a dozen calls.

"I'll call you back in an hour with the details," McCawley said as he hung up.

My smile threatened to cramp my cheeks.

The phone rang again before I could call Lawton with the news.

"This is Judy Steinberg with *Good Morning America*. We saw the UPI story. We'll book two airline tickets for tomorrow's show. What airport is closest to you?"

"Uh, sorry…we just committed to the *Tonight Show*." It suddenly occurred to me that I should have gotten McCawley's commitment in writing.

"You can't legally do that!" she screamed. Perhaps she thought I was an Iowa hick who didn't know how the media works.

"Sorry. When we give our word in Iowa, we stick to it. Let me talk to the *Tonight Show* and get back to you."

The phone didn't stop ringing long enough to call McCawley back. Several radio stations wanted the story, as did the *Today Show*, the *Miami Herald*, and the *Chicago Tribune*. And—who would have guessed—we got calls from a half dozen weirdos wanting to apply to be Cooper's fifty-first resident.

By the time McCawley called back, I was deep into second and third thoughts. Had my haste in agreeing to the *Tonight Show* prevented some other, maybe better interview opportunities? My doubts evaporated when he announced that our segment of the show might go "live" from Cooper with a split screen in LA. Wow, who ever thought Hollywood would come to Cooper!

McCawley arrived the next day to arrange for the production details, including a satellite uplink to feed interviews from Cooper back to his Burbank studios. I understood how satellite links worked, but I'd always assumed Iowa didn't have the technical capabilities to send a signal back. I assumed wrong.

I wanted McCawley to see the human side of the rural Midwest, so I arranged a potluck supper for the whole town at the Methodist church in Cooper.

He must have loved this down-home experience, because the next thing I knew, the producer had decided to broadcast the entire *Tonight Show* from Cooper. "We'll bring out Doc, Ed, Johnny, and the entire crew."

It sounded beyond great.

The best laid plans, of course...

When the folks in Corning, Iowa, read about it in the *Des Moines Register*, they clamored for the show to be broadcast from Corning, Johnny's hometown. That killed the Cooper broadcast idea, since Johnny didn't want to be the fodder for the rivalry between two small Iowa towns. Instead, the *Tonight Show* invited three of us—Lawton, a retired school bus driver named Myrtle Whitcher, and me—to Hollywood.

Boy, did they do it with style: airfare, limos, nice rooms at the Universal Sheraton, and our own dressing room—with our names and a star on the door—at the NBC Burbank studios. Johnny made us feel at ease, even coming to chat us up during makeup. What mattered far more than these perks, however, was that I got to "panel" on the *Tonight Show* at age twenty-nine…a dream many big-name comedians never experience. It was incredible sitting on the couch with Ed McMahon who, I swear, had Jack Daniels in his coffee cup.

And it was obvious Johnny wanted to be the fifty-first resident of Cooper.

By the night of the show, little tiny Cooper was all over the media. Lawrence Welk had applied for adoption, undoubtedly in response to the plethora of requests from Cooper townsfolk. Unsolicited applications had poured in as well: Henry "the Fonz" Winkler, Princess Grace of Monaco, Danny Thomas, and Mickey Mouse were among the celebrities who gave Johnny Carson a run for his money.

Of course, Johnny won by a landslide.

The media attention brought twelve thousand people to the July 11 centennial celebration, which was covered by *ABC*, *NBC*, *CBS*, *The Today Show*, and *Good Morning America*. The following Monday, Johnny mentioned Cooper on the show and thanked us for naming him the fifty-first citizen.

Cooper had become the "Mayberry" of Iowa.

P.S. Johnny never did do a show in Iowa, but he did one the following year in his "other" hometown of Norfolk, Nebraska. In my heart of hearts, I know the idea for the Nebraska show came from the Cooper event.

As for me, I learned that any idea—no matter how new, how small, or how ridiculous—can make a difference, if you are willing

The Tonight Show, 1981(L-R): Terry Rich, Myrtle Whitcher, Gerald Lawton

to put the effort into it. Who would have thought a small-town centennial would interest a national TV audience?

Another lesson was that you never know when an idea in one situation will trigger a solution to a problem in an entirely different context. The possibility of doing a live broadcast nationwide via a satellite uplink from Iowa seemed technologically remarkable at the time. It never dawned on me that it would inspire an amazingly profitable project at my employer, Heritage Communications, a few months later. And with that project, my career took off.

All because of an invitation to have a cup of coffee with an old farmer friend to kick around some ideas. And forty-three letters that failed to get a response from anyone.

And I don't even drink coffee!

Chapter 2

The Show Begins

I can't ever remember a time when I didn't have more ideas than I knew what to do with. Perhaps it was something in my DNA. Perhaps it was boredom with the endless routines of life on a farm. Whatever the reason, I was always on the lookout for a new and different way to do whatever it was I had to do.

Some of my ideas were good, some not, but I was always encouraged to "give it a shot."

My first creative venture—or at least the first one I remember—occurred one night in 1958 when my parents chaperoned a high school dance in Cooper. Although karaoke was still years into the future, the entertainment of choice that night was a phonograph and a microphone held up to willing singers.

About halfway through the evening, someone pulled me up on stage.

Did I mention that Elvis was hot in 1958? Pretending I was on Dick Clark's *American Bandstand*, I grabbed the mike and lip-synced to "Hound Dog." Local farmers, friends, and my family thronged around my feet and cheered me on. I loved every second of it. Only years later did I realize that I had been in the throes of an adrenalin rush.

The thing is…I was only in kindergarten.

It never occurred to me that a five-year-old couldn't entertain a high school audience.

It was pretty much the same story on our farm. I never stopped to ask how things were supposed to be done. I didn't mind hard work, but my heart was never in walking bean rows and ringing hogs…or in being the "owner" of an orphaned baby goat.

I got the baby goat because my dad wanted me to "learn to take responsibility." My job was to do bottle feedings before and after school. I liked the kid well enough, but geez, it was a pretty routine task. What's worse, it interfered with 4-H, softball, and my jazz band.

The delicate balance of mentoring
someone is not creating them in
your own image, but giving them the
opportunity to create themselves.

— *Steven Spielberg*

Terry Rich, 1968

My mind went into overdrive. What if I could run a pipe from the house to the barn and put a nipple on the barn end? Yowser, I could feed the goat from the house. Not exactly a standard solution, but it seemed to impress my mom and dad. I suggested calling my uncle, a plumber, and asking him to bring over the requisite length of pipe.

I suspect they knew it'd never get done, but they gave me an encouraging smile and said, "Sure, go ahead." My uncle's first reaction was that it was a good idea, but he pointed out that if the milk soured in the pipe, it would contain germs that might harm the baby goat.

I was back to walking across the farmyard to the barn. But that story still gets a good laugh.

As I think back to the feeding pipe, I realize that Dad always treated me as if I could do whatever I set out to do. But his faith in me took on a whole new dimension one Sunday during the Vietnam War. Our minister had to be away the Sunday after Christmas, and my dad asked if I'd stand in for him and deliver a sermon.

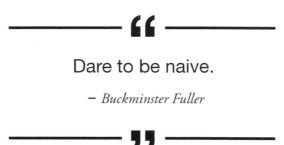

Dare to be naive.

– Buckminster Fuller

In retrospect, it strikes me as odd that a college student would be asked to preach to a rural congregation, many of whom were three times my age. But I thought I had something to say, so I jumped at the chance.

As an alternate delegate to the Democratic National Convention the previous summer, I'd been shocked by the abusive way the police treated the long-haired war protestors. At one point, while I was walking toward the convention center, I'd been shoved off the sidewalk by a baton-wielding cop for no reason that I could think of other than he thought I looked like one of the protesters.

That Sunday in Cooper, I intended to bring national politics to rural Iowa…to shake up a farm community with predominantly conservative social beliefs.

And I did.

Wearing a long, hippie-looking wig, I related the story of the Miami police tactics in painful detail, sharing my own reaction to what I thought was abusive and unreasonable behavior on the part of the police. I figured Mom would be a bit embarrassed. Even so, I wasn't prepared for the expressions that settled on the faces of many of the parishioners, including family friends. I could almost hear them thinking, "Poor Bud. How awful that his son has turned out like that."

Had I goofed?

As I'd planned, I ended the speech with, "And if you don't like today's generation, I guess I could do this!" and took off the wig. Slow chuckles led to knee-slapping laughter, as people decided that "that ornery kid, Terry" had been making a joke.

By the end of the service, I was back as a member in good standing of a very tight-knit community that liked to argue the issues but would always have your back in time of need.
Even today, the old folks remind me of that performance whenever I attend a church service in Cooper.

By the time I headed off to Iowa State University (ISU), I knew I was good at math and imagined I'd follow in my brother-in-law's footsteps…maybe even earn a PhD by solving a math problem that had never been solved before.

15

It was not to be.

After a year of soul-deadening "axiom and theorem" exercises to prove that one was not equal to zero, I was bored. I needed a real-world challenge.

---------------- **"** ----------------

You can study government and politics in school, but the best way to really understand the process is to volunteer your time.

– *Rob McKenna*

---------------- **"** ----------------

Fortunately, two significant challenges were waiting on my doorstep.

The first was politics. My parents were big Democrats and active in the community. While my parents cared about the issues, they thought the social impact of being involved was just as important, and they encouraged all three of their kids to volunteer on a regular basis. By the time I got to Iowa State, my grassroots politicking included senior class president and president of the county 4-H.

When the opportunity came to run for ISU freshman student president, I raised my hand and won. The job didn't have much authority, but it proved to be a splendid platform for networking with student leaders, many of whom became long-term friends and business associates. Being in student government also enhanced my appreciation for both the academic and administrative issues at a large public university.

On a somewhat loftier plane, I jumped into the spirit of the 1972 national election in my junior year. With my background, it seemed natural to attend the state Democratic convention. I thought it would be fun to see how delegates to the National Democratic Convention were selected.

Who would have thought that, as a nineteen-year-old, I might be one of them?

But as was my wont, I decided to break ranks with my fellow students, most of whom were backing George McGovern "What the heck," I thought, "I'll go for Hubert Humphrey."

Imagine my surprise when a little old man from Des Moines grabbed my elbow and said, "How'd you like to go to Miami? We need someone young to counter this McGovern vote."

"Uh, OK."

Next thing I knew I was an alternate delegate to the Miami convention in July. The first night, an unknown voice on the telephone instructed me to "go to the Hilton's ballroom. Bring two credentials. Come alone..."

Oh, the intrigue! I loved it.

When I arrived, there were only five people, all under the age of twenty-five, in the room. I was the youngest by several years. Out of nowhere, Hubert Humphrey materialized. "How are we going to get the young people to come to our side?" he wanted to know.

---------------- **"** ----------------

I consider my ability to arouse
enthusiasm among men the greatest
asset I possess. The way to develop
the best that is in a man is by
appreciation and encouragement.

– *Charles Schwab*

---------------- **"** ----------------

Oh man…here I was, at nineteen, strategizing with a former
vice president of the United States about taking the youth vote away
from McGovern. For the next hour, we discussed issues significant
to nineteen- to twenty-five-year-olds, most of whom were in college
or just entering the job market. Vietnam was high on our list, but
we also talked about jobs, freedom of expression, and whether Mc-
Govern was too liberal. The best part was strategizing about how to
convince other delegates that Humphrey was "the man."

Humphrey was energetic and listened attentively. His encouraging smiles and evident appreciation for our ideas made me feel I
was actually helping to elect the president of the United States.

It was a heady experience. I returned to my senior year primed
to run for student body president, pretty much assuming I'd continue to have an audience as long as I was willing to volunteer and
speak out. After all, I'd never lost an election, and we had a great
campaign slogan: "Is there really a better choice?" How could I fail?

Easily, as it turned out.

Iowa State University, 1973

Cocky with my own success, I didn't put in the effort to organize supporters the way I had as a freshman. As a "dorm geek" challenging candidates from the fraternity system, I decided on a running mate who seemed to be a hotshot in his fraternity. I learned too late that he was not as influential as he'd led me to believe. He couldn't—or wouldn't—mobilize the Greek vote.

———— **"** ————

Some people dream of success... others wake up and work hard at it.

– Author Unknown

———— **"** ————

Obviously, the rest of the student body thought there was a better choice as well.

I was devastated. But I learned a valuable lesson—that if I wanted to succeed, I had to be committed and funnel all my energy into whatever I was doing. I couldn't sit back and expect something to happen just because I wanted it.

The fact was that most of my energy during the election campaign had been devoted to my other big challenge—broadcasting (except we called it radio and TV back then).

My fascination with radio and TV began in my freshman year, when I heard about a DJ job at the college radio station, KPGY. My volunteer hand shot up. It looked way more interesting than being a math major.

———— **"** ————

I'd rather be a failure at something I love than a success at something I hate.

– George Burns

———— **"** ————

That radio job was, in retrospect, a watershed moment in my life. It taught me that radio is a theatre of the mind. As a DJ, I got to perform on a whole new stage. I got to relive the adrenaline rush of that Elvis moment almost every day.

Not long after I took the DJ job, I heard one of my classmates bragging about how exciting his TV/ radio class was. The way he described it, I could perform *and* make a living at the same time.

Whoa—I was in. In a nanosecond, I switched from math to speech / telecommunicative arts.

I wish I could say that I gave the decision to switch majors a lot of thought, I didn't. The idea that I might be able to earn a living as a radio or TV personality was tantalizing, but I had no idea what that meant in terms of a career. All I knew was that I wanted to do something that was a lot more fun than math.

═══ Chapter 3 ═══

Another Door Opens

For the next three years, I studied under the idiosyncratic and highly creative Dr. Charles Connolly. Like my dad, he was quick to compliment, slow to criticize, and always interested in his students' accomplishments. And perhaps more significantly, he dared his students to be creative—to do something no one else had done. He knew how to have fun and motivate people at the same time.

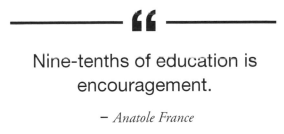

Nine-tenths of education is encouragement.

– Anatole France

Connolly provided lots of opportunities for a neophyte dreamer. For an internship in my sophomore summer, I set up a 4-H radio station at the local Greene County Fair. Pretty small potatoes, really, but the middle school students—with only a microphone, a turntable, and a speaker—had a ball pretending to be real DJs. The farmers and pigs were more than a little shaken by the rock and roll sounds.

Another awesome gig was being PR director for Kalidoquiz, a radio quiz show that was part of the annual spring festival at ISU. While KPGY normally had fewer than one hundred people listening, we got thousands on the Kalidoquiz weekend. The student management team organized dorms and fraternities to stay up all night for a radio trivia contest. Free food and a trophy were at stake. The DJ—that would be me—would ask a question, and while the next record played, the students had to figure out the answer. I was stunned to realize that students were stationed in the library and calling all over the United States to find out the answers. (Nope, Google hadn't been invented.)

A man must be big enough to admit his mistakes, smart enough to profit from them, and strong enough to correct them.

– John C. Maxwell

Some of our ideas worked better than others. A high—and low—point came the night we posed this question: *"In the town of Rippey, Iowa, the Methodist church has a bell in its driveway. What's the number on the bell?"*

At 2:30 in the morning, some two hundred cars headed for this little town of three hundred people, looking for the church. The town marshal had no idea what was coming. It was great fun, but I learned another good lesson: always contact the local authorities before pulling this kind of stunt. (Where was Chris Christie when we needed him?)

Not surprisingly, the college administrators had some strong words for us, but the dressing down didn't last long. No damage had been done, and the townsfolk had a great story for many years to come.

❝

Do you wait for things to happen, or
do you make them happen yourself?
I believe in writing your own story.

– *Charlotte Eriksson*

❞

KPGY was only a college radio station, but the format gave me a lot of room to experiment with unconventional programming ideas, even as I was learning the art and science of radio broadcasting.

Another watershed moment came my junior year when I went to New York as a student registrant to the National Association of

Broadcasters. Using my farm boy "everyone is a friend" manner, I struck up a conversation with the director of *ABC Evening News*. "Want to come by tomorrow and see the broadcast?" he said.

"Yep." What else could I say?

Standing in that ABC News control room, I knew I wanted to be a TV director. I liked having screen time, but even more, I wanted to be the guy who runs the show.

I was too eager try my hand at production to wait for my senior class project under Connolly: producing one show for the local ABC affiliate. When I got back to campus, I hooked up with Tom Wilhite, an exceptionally creative dude on ISU's student film committee. In our last two years, we produced four shows, each of which included a full jazz band, singers, dancers, and a live studio audience.

The adrenalin rush was unbelievable.

For three years, under Connolly's tutelage, I poured my energy into learning communication techniques. The more time I spent with TV and radio, the more invigorated I became. Long before I graduated, I knew broadcasting was my calling.

Connolly's real contribution to my career, however, was not in the technical aspects of radio and TV, but in his approach to creating an innovative environment.

Instruction does much, but encouragement does more.

– Johann Wolfgang von Goethe

Perhaps the most important thing that Connolly gave me was an understanding of creativity as a concept. People had always told me that I had a lot of imagination, but until I met him, I viewed creativity as a talent, like perfect pitch, something that you were born with…or not. Under Connolly, I began to see how creativity could, with the right kind of training and experience, be developed, nurtured, and disciplined.

First and foremost was Connolly's consistent pattern of providing encouragement and reassurance, no matter how cockamamie your idea sounded. There was no mistaking his genuine interest in his students and their ideas.

Another foundation stone of creativity, in Connolly's view, was that many of the greatest innovations come from building onto other people's ideas and applying old ideas in a new way.

---

ff

Our most original compositions are composed exclusively of expressions derived from others

– Alexander Graham Bell

jj

At one point, for example, Connolly challenged a group of graduate students to develop a better and cheaper methodology of conducting the annual audience surveys required by the FCC. Rating firms typically charged $5,000–$10,000 per year. One of the student ideas—to hire housewives to make the telephone survey calls from home—brought the cost down to $500–$1,000 per year.

Telephone surveys were hardly a new idea in the 1970s, but Connolly's class adapted the concept in a compelling way. By marketing it to TV stations, Connolly made his first million within two or three years. His ability to monetize a good idea made him even more credible to me.

An important lesson in this context was his insistence on not worrying about getting credit for a good idea. In one of his classes, I "invented" a plastic soda can opener so that flight attendants wouldn't break fingernails. I thought it was awesomely cool and was afraid someone would steal my idea before I could do something with it. When I shared my anxiety with Connolly, he laughed good-humoredly. "If someone steals your idea, it's validation that it was a good idea. Just go get another one."

And last but hardly least was his advice to avoid what he called the "Nomans"—the folks who are always ready to diss a new idea, to say, "*No, man*, we just don't do it that way."

Chapter 4

Fate Steps In

In April 1974, as I faced the daunting prospect of entering the work force, fate arrived in the person of Jim Cownie, the twenty-eight-year-old president of a one-town cable company in Des Moines. Cownie was a guest lecturer at the weekly job opportunity seminar for TV majors in their senior year.

I won't kid you. I was there that day because I still hadn't gotten around to applying for a real job. First of all, the kind of long-range planning that led many of my buddies to get glamorous job offers in broadcast TV and the movies was not my style.

Then too, my two off-the-cuff attempts at job hunting had not been encouraging. Midway through my senior year, I'd given an "air-check" tape from KPGY to the program director for KIOA-AM, the biggest rock station in Des Moines. Without even listening to it, he said dismissively, "You don't have the voice or the personality to ever work here." That really stung.

Remember that sometimes not
getting what you want is a wonderful
stroke of luck.

– Dalai Lama XIV

Later that spring, ISU's athletic department recommended Tom Wilhite and me as candidates for a job as ABC college football sideline reporters. Jim Lampley landed the job, and we got the "sorry" letter.

I was totally defeated.

Cownie was there because he needed a part-time intern to help with the upcoming election to approve bringing cable TV to Ames, Iowa. His company, Hawkeye Cablevision (later Heritage Communications), wanted to extend its cable franchise to Ames. Since Iowa required each city that intended to award a cable franchise to hold an election, Cownie was looking for a student with an interest in media and a background in politics to marshal the ISU student vote for the upcoming election.

It was dead obvious he was talking about me, so I raised my hand. Cable—still an emerging technology—wasn't as sexy as broadcast radio, TV, or movies, but I figured I could have some fun with the franchise vote and make a little money at the same time.

While the vote for the city of Ames as a whole failed, the student turnout was a stunning 90 percent in favor. I'd like to think it was because I worked hard—far harder than I'd worked for my own election to student government—to get the endorsement of my TV and radio buddies, including leaders in Greek and residential housing.

Our pitch was that the university's TV station—the dreaded "establishment"—was against the cable award, so students should, of course, be for it. It was like saying Instagram must be better than Facebook…since all the old people are now using Facebook.

A few days after the vote, Cownie called to say he was impressed with my creativity, energy, and work ethic. To my surprise, he asked if I'd be interested in coming to work for Hawkeye.

"Sure," I said.

I had no idea what I was getting myself into. In 1974, cable TV was a new technology that appealed primarily to rural households located too far away to get network broadcasts with their home antennas.

"

Luck is not as random as you think. Before that lottery ticket won the jackpot, someone had to buy it.

— *Vera Nazarian*

"

To make matters worse, Hawkeye Cablevision was a new kid on a new block, and their infrastructure was pretty basic. They could retransmit the four major networks (ABC, CBS, NBC, and Public Television) and two out-of-state independent TV stations.

They also owned a few black-and-white cameras to produce local content (e.g., school board and city council meetings), but they had no significant entertainment programs.

If viewers could get the network stations for free, why would they want to pay for cable? Could Hawkeye really make this idea work?

On the other hand, I had no other offers. And it did sound like fun.

On my first day, I reported to Bill Riley, the head of programming. By then, Riley was a well-known Iowa TV personality, largely due to his state fair talent TV show. This popular annual show was a cross between *American Idol* and *America's Got Talent*, but for kids. Local contests in towns across Iowa produced one hundred winners who showcased their talents at the Iowa State Fair. As a member of the Jefferson High School Jazz Band, I got to perform on his stage in my senior year in high school.

For a high school kid, the state fair show was the experience of a lifetime. For a college kid who couldn't seem to find a job, working for Riley was a dream come true.

Treat a man as he is and he will remain as he is. Treat a man as he can and should be, and he will become as he can and should be.

– *Stephen R. Covey*

Riley soon became my mentor, and I still think of him as an outstanding manager, someone who always saw the best in people and always had a word of encouragement.

He certainly knew how to inspire me. Moments after I arrived that first day, he informed me that my job as a "producer/director" was to think up ways to get people to watch cable TV.

Archie the Clown (Terry Rich) with Bill Riley, 1975

"It's easy," I said (like I knew what I was talking about). "Do what the radio stations do…put on a morning TV show with live music and prizes."

He took me at my word (like he believed I knew what I was talking about) and let me create a TV video show to run from 6:30 to 8:30 a.m.

For the next two years, my workday began with playing records and giving away prizes. Not only was I the DJ, but I also did every-thing else—directing (including setups for the remote-controlled camera), audio, and interviews. Most interviews were by phone, but I was in my element when Rosalynn Carter showed up to pro-mote her husband's presidential campaign.

In addition, I was part of a team that produced several other shows. In the afternoon, we played cable TV bingo and gave away prizes, mostly stuff that the station traded for advertising. The old ladies loved us, and we got live call-ins from winners. That show taught me to think on my feet—we never knew what outrageous thing a caller might say.

Another cool cable program was reading the Sunday comics to the kids. We adapted the idea from a famous routine by Chicago Mayor Richard J. Daley, who read the comics over the radio during a newspaper strike. We asked our cable families to lay out the Sunday comics in front of them. A buddy worked and voiced a hand puppet of a Saint Bernard as I read the comics to the kids from the paper. Our goal was to help teach kids to read as well as to entertain.

These were among the earliest attempts by cable companies to create original content targeted to local audiences. In the pre-sat-ellite days, it was the only—and not very successful—way to make cable appeal to a wider audience. But these shows were among the first interactive media on cable. It meant we could listen to our customers. We learned a lot from them, and we had fun doing it.

I didn't get paid much, but those shows fired up my already blazing ambition to be a TV director. Then too, Cownie assured me that my stock and stock options might be worth something someday. *Yeah right.*

After a year with Riley, I switched to ad sales manager. I continued to host the early morning TV DJ gig and also to produce shows—both local community activities and regional cable sales promotions—all in search of unique ways to get and keep new cable subscribers.

1975(L-R): Bill Riley, Terry Rich, Terri Cropp

Selling ads provided my first real-world experience with the "Nomans" that Connolly had warned about. In one instance, I was thrilled to snag a customer willing to pay $50 in advertising fees (decent money in 1975) if their commercial ran as part of a video-tape of a local high school football game.

"We'd make money if we do it with one camera and somebody to do the play-by-play," I suggested in a staff meeting.

"No way," said the production manager. "We need at least two cameras and a full crew."

Remember, man does not live by bread alone. Sometimes he needs a little buttering up.

– John C. Maxwell

I screwed up my courage and offered to produce the show my-self, with one camera and my buddy, the late night master control operator. To my surprise, I got the go-ahead. The broadcast was pretty crude, but I figured out that the key to success was to put as many local faces and names on the show as possible. The players, their families, and the community loved it!

That week, I sold enough ads for a full package of six games.

Barely a year later, I found myself responsible for selling new cable services to individual households rather than selling com-mercials—business-to-customer rather than business-to-business.

I was tasked with building a sales and marketing team. I was determined to hire people who actually believed in the Heritage mission as much as I did.

But there I was, knowing nothing whatsoever about selling door-to-door. For six months, I spent my days in the office developing marketing strategies and my evenings ringing doorbells. Door-to-door sales are tough under the best of circumstances. Our rule of thumb was that if you hit one hundred addresses in a night, you might sell two or three subscriptions.

People don't know what they want
until you show it to them.

— Steve Jobs

And 1976 was not the best of circumstances in terms of sales. Most people were perfectly content with the existing—free—network channels on their TVs. The local programs and promotions that Heritage produced didn't have broad audience appeal. We also offered a few premium channels, but those cost even more. How do you sell Mom and Pop on a cable subscription for TV programs they don't want anyway?

Selling door to door taught me perseverance, but it left me with the same sinking feeling in my gut that I'd had writing a term paper on the mathematical relationship between one and zero.

I heaved a sigh of relief when I got transferred to operations, where I oversaw the development of new cable systems, first in Marshalltown and then around Central Iowa (including Ames, Iowa, where we had lost the election some five years before). Expansion relied heavily on door-to-door sales as cable capacity was built out in each new neighborhood, but now these one-on-one sales were someone else's responsibility.

I was several years into that job when I received that fateful call from Jim McCawley.

Did I mention it changed my life?

Those who have succeeded at anything and don't mention luck are kidding themselves.

– Larry King

A couple months after the Cooper Centennial, I moved to the corporate marketing department, where I was in charge of "promotions." (Cooper helped, wouldn't you think?) Heritage's marketing and management staff met with our HBO affiliate to explore ways to promote HBO. Heritage had purchased HBO movies for several years, but their appeal increased dramatically once the movies were available from a satellite feed instead of physical reels sent via US mail. HBO wanted a bigger audience, and Heritage wanted the larger revenue stream that came with the premium channels.

I remembered McCawley's idea about up-linking the *Tonight Show* by satellite and broadcasting it nationwide. If NBC could do it from Cooper, why couldn't we produce a cable sales promotion in Des Moines and transmit it to the Heritage cable systems across the United States via a satellite uplink?

I proposed that once a year we preempt time on a dozen or so of our cable channels to show HBO movies for free. In between the movies, we would transmit (via satellite uplink) a national "telethon" to promote HBO subscriptions. As a marketing strategy, it was akin to the Home Shopping Network, but for premium cable programs.

"

If everyone says you are wrong, you're one step ahead. If everyone laughs at you, you're two steps ahead.

– Charles Chic Thompson

"

The Heritage marketing folks loved the idea, but my HBO counterpart roundly rejected it. He didn't believe for a moment that a little town in Iowa could do a national promotion using a satellite uplink. (Darn those "Nomans"!)

The programming folks at Heritage urged me to keep the pressure on HBO, as the combo of previews and ad promotions in multiple cities would mean very big bucks. Two months later, after the fifth rejection, I finally got a meeting with HBO's engineering VP. When I wrapped up what seemed an increasingly futile pitch, he offered eight simple words: "Sure, when do you want the uplink there?"

Here it was—my college dream come true. I was the "executive producer" of a nationwide promotion hawking cable subscriptions. Even better, I got to be the "talent" (the guy with the clean-shaven face) on a TV show. It was a lot more fun than selling door to door. I reached out to my old professor, Chuck Connolly, for his technical expertise. In the meantime, our marketing department created a promotion called "Gold Star Weekend," including one million direct mail pieces to be sent to customers to promote the event. Two weeks prior to the first broadcast, Jim Cownie stormed into a staff meeting. "Who the f**k came up with this HBO satellite deal? We're sending out one million direct mail pieces and we've never done this before?"

I acknowledged I was the one with the crazy idea. When I explained how the promotion would work, Cownie smiled. "Well, good luck. Just make it work."

Yes, my career took off because I had a cup of coffee in Cooper. But it also took off because I worked for a company that encouraged me to try out new ideas.

That first weekend we sold enough cable and HBO subscriptions to add nearly $2 million to our bottom line for the year, at a cost of less than $100,000 for production and marketing.

Connolly had been right. Some of the most successful initiatives come from taking other people's ideas and adapting them to a new environment.

By the time we ran the first HBO promotion, I was the special events manager, a new title in the marketing department under Dale Parker.

Parker and I made a great team over the next nine years. He was good at defining strategic initiatives with an emphasis on the nuts and bolts of basic marketing. We had a dire need to train our customer service and technical personnel in selling and customer satisfaction. Though "lean and mean," we had an exceptional team of corporate marketing staff to support our efforts.

By contrast, I was good at execution and communications with the field. He taught me to use my ideas to capitalize on my strengths and work with people who could fill in for my weaknesses. He also taught me that my farm boy image needed a little polishing if I was going to go out and rub shoulders with the "big boys."

At the time I started in marketing, special events were mostly local content shows and cable promotions, the sort I'd been producing for years.

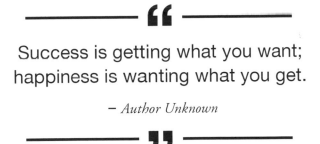

Success is getting what you want;
happiness is wanting what you get.

– Author Unknown

The HBO preview was a game changer. The idea of nationwide promotions caught on, and it wasn't long before Heritage was doing promotions for new channel launches like Showtime or Disney. As with HBO, we produced these shows ourselves, but increasingly set them in hot spots around the country—Hollywood, Walt Disney World, ESPN, CNN, MGM Grand in Las Vegas. We also featured celebrities from the world of entertainment and sports— CNN's Larry King, CSPAN's Brian Lamb, E Entertainment's Suzanne Sena, and QVC host Dan Wheeler.

On a typical weekend, we'd sell cable services to thirty to forty thousand households. Over the next nine years, those annual previews added $12–$14 million to Heritage's net worth.

I loved every moment of it. I mean, really. How many start-up companies have the fun that Hollywood programming provides?

Ted Turner with Terry Rich, 1984

We were invited to everything—sporting events by ESPN and FOX, music events by MTV and VH-1, movie and grand opening events by HBO and Disney.

But I also thrived on some of the less flashy special events. One of my favorites occurred in 1984, shortly after Heritage bought the Dallas cable system from Warner-Amex Communications. Warner had awful service and left us with a huge PR problem. The marketing folks wanted a quick PR stunt to show our sincerity.

Once again, I reached back into my storehouse of other people's good ideas…this time one I'd seen at a small cable system in Pennsylvania.

On Halloween, our cable service staff donned Halloween costumes and delivered candy to disabled children in Dallas who could not go out to trick-or-treat themselves. It was great turning my creativity to doing something good for someone in need. It was even better when the local paper delivered a top-of-the-fold editorial, touting how cool Heritage was to do this Halloween promotion.

Life was good.

And then, in 1986, everything changed.

By then, Heritage was one of the ten largest cable operators in the United States with a million customers in some four hundred communities across twenty-two states. Heritage also owned radio and TV stations, operated the second-largest billboard company in the country, and owned a major trade show display company as well as the world's largest movie projection screen company. Our stock was listed on the NYSE.

It seems that a money manager for the Bass Brothers thought our stock was undervalued and started buying. To thwart a hostile take-over, Jim Hoak, Heritage's CEO, decided to partner with another large cable company to do a leveraged buyout. It had worked for RJR Nabisco. Why wouldn't it work for Heritage?

In early 1987, Heritage partnered with the cable division of TCI, the nation's largest cable company. The deal called for TCI to cash out our management team, but not take corporate control for three to five years. The Heritage management team received "golden handcuffs" in the form of continued profit sharing. There was a huge financial upside if we could drive the value of the company up before TCI took control.

Virtually overnight, the aura of Heritage changed. Now our goal was maximizing profits and building cash value rather than developing new and innovative approaches to marketing and programming. Expenses were scrutinized, and investment opportunities got short shrift. Risk-taking just didn't happen.

A good director creates an
environment, which gives the actor
the encouragement to fly.

— *Kevin Bacon*

We made a lot of money in the end, but it just wasn't the same.

Those last few years under TCI made it clear how rich a heritage my first thirteen years had offered. I'd had the privilege of working with what was a close-to-perfect leadership team during a time of innovation. Jim Hoak, the CEO, "dared to dream." A Des Moines native, Yale undergrad, and Stanford law grad, Jim was intrigued with the new frontier of cable television and decided to partner with his old school buddy, Jim Cownie, to start a cable company. A visionary and serial entrepreneur, Hoak was on the leading edge of many of the new developments in the cable industry.

I'll always remember his prediction in the late 1970s that we'd have satellite programming within a year. He got a big laugh from a skeptical management team, but within six months, Heritage was the second satellite affiliate of HBO.

The other half of the team, Jim Cownie, the president, "dared to act." The super-athletic Cownie was a natural leader: he had drive, a desire to succeed, and a contagious smile. Like Connolly at ISU, Cownie understood that people thrive on respect, encouragement, and positive reinforcement. Although he was notoriously tight with money, Cownie gave his people the freedom to bring their best into play. My career would have been very different if he had vetoed the $100,000 expenditure for that first HBO promotion.

From my first day, I had been part of a team tasked with creating a new industry. Every day, we faced problems that no one else had ever solved. The pressure to come up with a better mousetrap was intense, particularly in those first few very rocky years, and staff meetings usually included heated debates. We saw Hoak and Cownie argue, but when the discussion was over, they would laugh and smile. We worked our tails off, not so much for the company but for those two men. We could see how much they cared, and we didn't want to disappoint them.

> ## ❝
>
> ## Happiness happens on the way to success.
>
> *— Terry Rich*
>
> ❞

We had a lot of crazy ideas and took a lot of chances. Some failed. But those that worked—like the HBO previews—worked big.

Throughout it all, I had fun. My time with Heritage stands as a testament to the old adage that you will be most successful if you focus your energy on what you love and what you're good at. My farm boy manner made me a natural marketer, skills I could have put to good use in any industry. But I doubt that any other industry would have given me the depth of satisfaction I got from the world of radio and TV—from producing the national telethons to rubbing shoulders with the best in the business.

1982 First Satellite Preview Uplink from Iowa, Des Moines Iowa
(L-R) All from HBO: Frank Hughes, Michael Andrasani, Dave Rodriquez, Mark Walsh, Les Read
Heritage Communications: Jim Cownie, Terry Rich, Charles Connolly, Dale Parker, Bill Riley

Chapter 5

Building on My Heritage

During the first month of full TCI management in 1991, I was offered a job as head of programming in Colorado. It meant moving to Denver with my wife and young children. It meant working for a company that was not known for their friendly corporate culture.

I declined.

It wasn't an easy decision, but there I was, not even forty and successful beyond anything I could have imagined. After converting my stock to cash and socking away my share of the profits in the last few years, I had all the money I thought I'd ever need. Heck, maybe it was time to retire.

I tried golfing for a couple weeks, but that bored me even more than proving that one was not equal to zero.

There had to be something I could do. I'd always liked to gamble. Starting my own business sounded like an interesting and different sort of gamble.

—————— " ——————

You have to leave the city of your
comfort and go into the wilderness
of your intuition. What you'll
discover will be wonderful. What
you'll discover is yourself.

— *Alan Alda*

—————— 🟊🟊 ——————

Heritage had a reputation for employing fair and honest people, so it made sense to leverage my marketing reputation, production expertise, and love of being on stage. And strange as it seems, given a decade of successful promotions for old standbys like HBO and newer channels like The Disney Channel, no one else had picked up on the idea. If I decided to build a business out of preview promotions, I would have no competition.

When I asked Cownie if I could use the Heritage name and start Heritage Marketing, he replied, "Heck, put your name on it. How about 'Rich Heritage'?"

I figured I could afford to invest $10,000, with the self-imposed rule that I'd call it quits if I had to put in more. I'd only bet what I could lose. What I didn't know was that being a successful production and marketing guy for a conglomerate was not the same as running my own company.

I had a lot to learn about managing a business.

My first task at Rich Heritage (RHI) was to rustle up some customers. While I didn't want to work for TCI, it made sense to reach out to them, as they were the cable system I knew best. They produced their own programs, along with retransmitting premium channels like HBO. Free previews seemed like an obvious pitch.

I did some brainstorming with a telemarketing vendor for TCI. Mike suggested we submit a joint proposal; his company would handle direct mail and the phone bank, and RHI would produce a promotional telethon. I put together a $125,000 proposal for the SVP of operations.

I sat by while Mike pitched a RHI production to the SVP. "Terry's previews have gotten a lot of new HBO subscribers. It would make a great fall promotion for TCI."

"How much?" the SVP asked.

"Two hundred thousand," replied my telemarketing guru.

"Let's do it," exclaimed the SVP. We arranged to get together in two weeks to finalize the details.

Holy smokes. Rich Heritage had just done its first deal. On the other hand, it looked like Mike had just made $75,000 off my project, in addition to his mail and phone campaign.

When I confronted him on the way out, I got my first big lesson in running a business. I'd forgotten about overhead—things like office rental and insurance. I'd never given any thought to that stuff at Heritage, as that was someone else's responsibility. Now it was all mine. Without Mike's intervention, I would have been bankrupted before I got started.

Back in Denver two weeks later, I made sure I had time for breakfast—a cinnamon roll, hash browns, and a Diet Coke—at McDonald's. I'd been early for the first TCI meeting, so I had stopped at McDonald's to kill time. Since it brought me luck at the first meeting, I thought I'd try it again.

When Mike and I arrived, the SVP's office was empty. Moments later, the door flew open and our host stormed in. "That goddamn head of Encore has us in trouble," he screamed at no one in particular.

It seemed that TCI had just established an in-house premium movie channel called Encore. TCI had planned to force distribution and add $1 to every customer's bill, a strategy many viewed as an illegal "negative option." The attorneys general in several states had filed injunctions to stop the automatic increase in cable fees, thereby forcing TCI to do a positive sell on every customer.

When he calmed down a bit, the SVP glanced over at me. "What are you doing here?"

"Remember we decided to do an HBO preview promotion this fall?" I said.

I've found that what most people call luck is often little more than raw talent combined with the ability to make the most of opportunities.

– Timothy Zahn

He went silent for what seemed like five minutes but was probably only ten seconds. I knew the HBO idea was dead in the water.

And then, the fates made their appearance. "Why couldn't we do this promotion for Encore?" he asked.

"We could," I said.

"You said two hundred thousand dollars for three days. What would it cost to do an Encore promotion for four weeks?"

Now that was a big number. Satellite time. Production time. Crews and talent 24/7. Even as I threw out a price—nearly a million dollars—that would cover direct costs, overhead, and a good return for my expertise and risk, I was in shock. It was more money than my dad ever saw in his lifetime.

"Perfect. Have it ready by next Friday," he shot back.

I had to force myself to breathe. Two five-minute conversations with one guy and Rich Heritage was cash-flowed for a long, long time. And cash-flowed without much risk (at least that's what I thought), since TCI would be funding it at every step.

Breakfast at McDonald's before a big sales meeting became a tradition.

It was only when I got back to Des Moines that I realized I had nothing in writing, just a handshake. I would have been bankrupted several times over if this project had gone south, but I didn't know enough to worry. As it turned out, TCI sent me half the money in four days and the balance within a week after the promotion ended. Good ideas, fair pricing, and honest handshakes worked.

Ten days later, the first Encore promotion was transmitted into more than fifteen million homes across the country, with a target of picking up five hundred thousand new customers. In fact, the promotion convinced over a million customers to buy a new movie channel that was less expensive than HBO.

Even before the first TCI promotion was finished, I knew I needed help. I had lined up other celebrities as spokespeople for some of the promotions, and it was increasingly obvious that I couldn't do the marketing, be the talent, and also run the day-to-day production business.

> **Diversity: the art of thinking independently together.**
>
> – *Malcolm Forbes*

And as I had seen in that first meeting with TCI, I wasn't a detail guy. RHI would never have survived if I hadn't hired Liz Gilman, a veteran TV producer of national training programs and broadcast shows. Liz was organized, thorough, and in touch with consumer trends. Her youth and distinctive visual graphic style provided much-needed diversity at RHI. She was RHI's only other employee. She and I did at least two dozen more preview promotions for TCI, all without a contract. I did wise up enough to get contracts with the other cable customers—Cox, Charter, Time Warner, AT&T, Comcast, and Adelphia. Over the next twelve years, RHI produced over 100 promotional telethons.

We continued to hire equipment, crews, and talent when and where we needed them—Orlando, Las Vegas, New York, LA, Denver, and New Orleans. We often benefitted from a neat barter arrangement. Rich Heritage got free or low-cost studio space and/or housing while the cable company got an extra dollop of PR from having the production crew on site.

The production I remember most was the preview-based sales gig for live pay per view boxing shows in Las Vegas. For twenty-four hours before each fight, we conducted interviews with celebrities and guests live from the Caesar's Palace pressroom. In between, we ran promos for a $39 cost of purchasing the pay per view event and even chatted with viewers who called to weigh in on the fight's outcome.

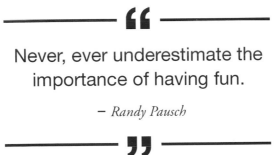

Never, ever underestimate the importance of having fun.

– Randy Pausch

This direct-to-the-customer service was one-on-one social media before social media was cool. Best of all, Liz and I got to be up close and personal at the three greatest heavyweight boxing matches I've ever witnessed—Bowe/Holyfield I, II, and III.

There it was again. Happiness happens on the way to success.

All because Johnny Carson liked the Cooper idea. And remember—forty-three of the forty-four letters I sent to lure some publicity show idea failed.

More than once during the RHI years, I had an itch to do something different. The national telethons were always fun, but they weren't much of a challenge. At one point, for example, I partnered with a couple buddies to build a radio station from scratch and sold it at a considerable profit a year later. I tackled several other projects as well, but generally viewed them as "sideline" businesses.

My perspective began to shift with the dot.com bust in 2000. A steady pace of consolidation in the cable industry was changing the way cable companies did business, and many of the new megacorporations preferred to do their own previews and promotions. When some of the new industry leaders began to have financial problems, I could see the handwriting on the wall.

Fate intervened once again.

It was a Friday in July 2002. We'd just completed a free preview weekend for Adelphia, a family-run public company that was now one of the top five US cable operators. Their marketing guy was great to work with, and they paid their bills promptly.

That day, Adelphia's $230,000 check for the final payment arrived in the morning mail. We deposited it in the bank by noon.

When I returned from lunch, Liz was standing in front of the TV. "Oh my God, Terry! Did you see who just got arrested?"

On CNN, John Rigas, Adelphia's chairman, was being led off to jail in handcuffs. He'd been accused of stealing funds from the company. By early the following week, Adelphia's bank accounts had been frozen.

My check cleared, but it was a wake-up call. The market I once thought I understood so well was turning into a zoo.

Liz and I had a great run, but the balance of risk and reward was no longer working for me. It was time to reconsider retirement.

═══ Chapter 6 ═══

A Different Kind of Zoo

The world as a zoo ceased to be a metaphor some months later when I got a phone call from an ex-governor of Iowa. "Would you be willing to try to turn the finances of the Des Moines zoo around?"

Well, that was about as far from the world of cable TV as you could get. On the other hand, I grew up raising animals. Were giraffes really that different from cows and pigs?

I had no idea. I'd been to the zoo twice with my kids, but despite growing up around farm animals, I had no real feel for, or interest in, the residents of the zoo.

But the trustees of the zoo weren't looking for someone to love the animals. They wanted someone who could sell the zoo to the citizens of Iowa. Heck, I'd sold cable TV when almost nobody needed it. I'd sold a small-town centennial celebration to the national media. How hard could it be to sell exotic animals doing exotic things?

Wow! A real-world problem looking for a solution.

I was in!

My first task was to find out why the zoo was losing so much money. My instinct was to blame it on two decades of politically driven decisions during the joint City of Des Moines/ Blank Park Zoo Foundation management. Now that control had been turned over to the foundation, I assumed that making money would be a whole lot easier.

It wasn't. I soon learned that the traditional business model for a zoo and many types of museums is inherently unsustainable.

You visit once as a child. Twenty-odd years later, you come a couple times with your own children. Another twenty years pass before you show up again, this time with grandchildren. This "generational" model requires significant municipal support and/or generous private donations.

By the time I joined, however, both the city and the donors had lost the will to keep propping the zoo up. My job was to improve the zoo's image and bring in more paying customers.

I reached out to the Meyocks Group, the zoo's pro bono ad agency, which came up with a new tagline: "Iowa's Wildest Adventure." Not long after that, the creative director of the Trilix Group, a competitor agency, weighed in with a more human angle coined by his son when he heard the "Wildest Adventure" commercial: "Do the zoo."

But these changes were cosmetic. A few sexy ads might bring in new visitors, but if they didn't like what they saw, they wouldn't come back a second time.

To succeed, the zoo needed an innovative approach that would appeal to demographic groups other than families with school age children. We needed customers who would come regularly and provide a consistent cash flow.

> **"**
>
> ## The great secret is that an orchestra can actually play without a conductor at all. Of course, a great conductor will have a concept and will help them play together and unify them.
>
> — *Joshua Bell*
>
> **"**

But how?

As I look back on how I grappled with this issue, I recalled a speech by Bill Rancic, an entrepreneur and frequent motivational speaker. "You don't have to do it all," he'd said. "Just be the conductor."

It was a terrific bit of advice. To conduct an orchestra, you don't need to know how to play a trumpet, a violin, or a clarinet. What you do need is the ability to pick good musicians and point them in the direction you want them to go. As the conductor, you get to decide whether to play loud or soft…when to speed up the tempo or slow it down…and who should play the solo.

But the musicians make the music.

His words took me back to my days as producer for HBO promotions. I loved being the "host" on those shows, but their ultimate success relied on getting the right celebrity guests, whether it was Mickey Mouse or Larry King.

My challenge was to harness the talents of zoo employees who were able—and maybe even eager—to go beyond the bureaucratic mind-set. My ace in the hole was that most people who work in a zoo love animals. Given half a chance, they'll do almost anything to improve conditions for their charges.

The orchestra metaphor was perfect...the zoo's staff really did want to make good music.

But as members of the city's union, they'd been living in a bureaucratic and politically charged environment for years. Morale had been sapped by constant threats of job cuts and the increasing disrepair of many of the animal facilities. New projects that would distract from animal care were certain to be received with suspicion or outright hostility.

I had a zoo full of "Nomans."

Never let a good crisis go to waste.

– Winston Churchill

I had no choice but to remind them that if we couldn't come up with ways to generate more revenue, the zoo would close. But I also emphasized the positive side of things—that for the first time, management and staff had full control of day-to-day operations. If we could produce more revenue, we could use it however we wanted.

I also repeated, again and again, that I needed their ideas to accomplish that.

Taking a lesson from my days at Heritage, I encouraged staff to bring any and all problems to me—in staff meetings, in one-on-one conversations, by e-mail, or sometimes a conversation in the hall. But I wanted their comments to be productive, so I insisted that any statement of a problem be accompanied by a proposed solution.

In the same vein, I encouraged zoo staff to share new ideas, no matter how farfetched they seemed. Invariably, I tried to push them even further by asking "how about…" or "what if…"

A confession here. You will almost certainly know if you've read this far that I'm a doer, not a planner. If there's an agenda for a meeting, I struggle to follow it. I'm sure some of the zoo folks found my management style frustrating, but there was a method to my madness.

The role of a creative leader is not to have all the Ideas; It's to create a culture where everyone can have ideas and feel that they are valued.

– *Ken Robinson*

First of all, it kept staff from falling back on "how it's always been done" and primed them to come up with and consider new ideas. Then too, their suggestions exponentially expanded my knowledge

Terry Rich at the Blank Park Zoo, 2007

of the zoo's operations. Last but not least, meetings enabled once-si-loed staff to learn about each other's projects and provided a forum to build a consensus for the projects staff cared about.

As it turned out, the zoo's staff generated a lot of terrific ideas.

One of the zanier suggestions—a zoo parade—came from Ryan Bickel, the zoo's marketing director. We recorded the comments of the current mayor, Shawn Johnson (the Olympic gymnast), and a dozen more celebrity friends of the zoo as they pretended to lead one of the animals down a very busy street in Des Moines.

During each break in the morning commuter radio show on a popular rock and roll radio station, the DJ turned to the parade.

We actually convinced thousands of listeners that wild animals were walking down a public road (shades of Kalidoquiz!).

Did I mention that the parade was held on April Fools' Day?

In keeping with the April Fools theme, the parade included three exotic red bats, which would be kept on exhibit at the zoo for a couple weeks before going back to Louisville, Kentucky. We pointed out that they had to be handled with special gloves. Their cage was a fifty-gallon drum covered with chicken wire and flagged with a sign that said "BEWARE: dangerous red bats."

Over the next three weeks, thousands of people came to the zoo to see those bats—three baseball bats painted red. As a bonus, we attached two baseballs to one of the bats and asked the adults if they knew which one was the male and which was the female. Everyone seemed ready to laugh at the joke. It created a whole new adult feeling about a venue that had been written off for years as the "kiddie" zoo.

Many ideas grow better when transplanted into another mind than in the one where they sprang up.

— Oliver Wendell Holmes

Another terrific idea was Zoo Brew, an adults-only evening event. Some of the staff had seen the concept at other zoos, but only as a fundraising device, where the focus was on the donors rather than the animals. Colleen Murphy, our special events co-ordinator, picked up on the idea and suggested several new twists. Make the event free to zoo members and cheap for the general public. Keep the animals out for the evening. Bring in musicians who'd appeal to twenty- and thirtysomethings.

It was another great idea just waiting to be adapted. But this time, the "Nomans" came out in force. "The animals have to go off exhibit at five p.m. The noise will disturb them. We can't have liquor in the park."

Staff concerns about the impact on the animals of longer exposure to noise and crowds were genuine. But it was also true that the zoo's already overworked and underappreciated staff didn't want to work in the evenings.

I couldn't blame them. On the other hand, the old playbook simply wasn't working.

It took Murphy several months to convince the animal care staff that the animals would not be harmed—and might benefit—from variations of routine. When Zoo Brew was grudgingly launched in the summer of 2004, we were thrilled to get four hundred people. Staff enthusiasm mounted as the crowd—and the zoo's revenues—grew over the summer, contributing funds for animal facilities as well as education and enrichment programs. It didn't hurt that the press acknowledged the success of the zoo's efforts, often above the fold of the local newspaper.

Ideas began to flow.

By 2009, the zoo had a stable and positive cash flow as well as a $12 million endowment fund that kicked out cash to tide us over during down weeks. Based on attendance numbers from the Iowa

Tourism Office, the zoo had become one of the most popular cultural attractions in Iowa.

The zoo was now poised to launch its strategic plan for expansion of the animal facilities and exhibits. The board's focus had shifted to fund-raising, including a major capital campaign for construction.

Both were well outside of my area of expertise and interest, and no one on my staff had any experience with large-scale zoo construction. I had done what I could do for the zoo. It was time for someone else to take the helm and for me to find another challenge.

When Ed Stanek, the director of the Iowa Lottery, retired, friends suggested that I apply for the job. I had second thoughts about working for a government agency. While the Iowa Lottery had generated nearly $1 billion in revenues for the state, the industry as a whole had matured. Innovation was infrequent and not altogether welcome. Management was expected to be acutely sensitive to the social impact (e.g., don't oversell...don't get people addicted). Every decision was scrutinized by the media and the legislature. One political or integrity mistake and you were toast. On the other hand, the job description emphasized marketing and promotion. How could I not be interested?

When I took over as CEO in February 2009, the political climate was toxic. In Iowa, senior staff were still reeling, politically and financially, from legislative action in March 2006 that banned the lottery's video poker machines. My charge from Governor Culver was to improve the lottery's image and grow existing lines of business. I hoped that my reputation at the zoo would allow me to befriend both sides of the political aisle.

Once again I had a lot to learn…but in a sense, I had a blank chalkboard on which to write the next chapter of the Iowa Lottery.

Having come from a world in which innovation and trial and error were encouraged, I instinctively explored new approaches to tried-and-true practices, policies, and game styles at the lottery. *Wonder what this game would look like in red? Can we give away an elephant? What about offering discounts at retail stores to customers who purchase a Powerball ticket?*

All fun ideas to contemplate.

I am always doing that which I cannot do, in order that I may learn how to do it

– Pablo Picasso

What I didn't realize was the stress I was creating for employees. Too often, staff left a meeting thinking all my ideas had to be executed—and to be done immediately. After a few months, the management staff demanded a "come-to-Jesus" meeting.

"All I wanted," I explained sheepishly, "was to pitch out ideas to consider. You can throw them if they have no value to you."

It took awhile for the management team to believe that I didn't expect every idea to be viewed as an order. Once they did, however, the group devised a way to manage the flow of ideas.

It was brilliant!

Henceforth, the subject line in memos and e-mails would define the desired response in one of three ways:

<u>Action Required</u> (roughly 20 percent of our e-mails): You're expected to follow up on the idea. Enough said.

<u>FYI</u> (used 30 percent of the time): Read and be aware of this for future discussions, but you don't have to do anything immediately.

<u>C.O.T.</u> (50 percent of our communication): "Consider or Throw Away." The feeling of the sender should be "Hey, I just wanted to get this idea off my chest before I forget it." The rules were simple:

No response is expected.

Heck, if you're busy, just hit delete.

If you have an idea and want to send it to me, go for it... but don't expect a response.

Iowa Lottery's Mary Neubauer, Local Bondurant, IA Powerball winners, Terry Rich 2012

There it was! C.O.T.—*the newest innovative idea created by need in my sixty-year existence.* Almost immediately, staff stress was reduced.

An unexpected fringe benefit of the C.O.T. solution was that it provided a "safe harbor" under Iowa's "Sunshine Laws" that allow anyone to file a Freedom of Information request. Since all work e-mails are considered public documents, the law discourages simple and direct e-mail communication by state employees.

By identifying e-mails as C.O.T.s, we reduced the odds of a news report that, for example, "the lottery plans to launch a new marijuana ticket." Of course, a reporter might write the story and check the facts later. But there's no doubt that C.O.T. improved the staff's communication—and out-of-the-box thinking.

Once we opened up the ideas tunnel for all to enjoy, we increased sales and profits for Iowa by over 30 percent ($28 million) in the 2013 fiscal year.

Chapter 7

Looking in the Rearview Mirror

When I was growing up, people were always saying I was creative. For years I thought it was a polite way of telling me I was a little bit crazy.

And I probably am a little bit crazy. I'm constantly coming up with ideas that people don't quite know what to do with...ideas that seem goofy or inappropriate or breach all the rules.

**If you obey all the rules,
you miss all the fun.**

– Katharine Hepburn

But you're reading this book because I've found ways to put a few good ideas into action. I mean, really, would anyone in Cooper, Iowa, have cared about my great PR idea if I hadn't headed off to the library and acted on it?

If you're looking for ways to *create an innovative environment*, here's my advice: **Dare to Dream and Dare to Act**.

Just don't try to do them both at the same time!

Dare to Dream

It is important to recognize that creativity does not require genius. Indeed, research suggests that, beyond a certain level, intelligence does not correlate with creativity.[1]

> **"**
>
> Einstein was asked which is more important, creativity or knowledge? His answer: "Creativity, because knowledge is finite."
>
> **"**

What creativity requires is a willingness to let your mind wander, to ponder what would happen if…

It requires the ability to daydream.

——————— 66 ———————

It is the ability to spot the potential
in the product of connecting things
that don't ordinarily go together
that marks out the person who is
truly creative.

– Phil Beadle

——————— 99 ———————

Indeed, research conducted by the legendary psychologist Jerome Singer indicated that daydreaming is one of the essential elements of a healthy and productive mind, and he found a strong correlation between daydreaming and creativity. Singer's work is validated by more recent studies[2] that demonstrate the benefits, including planning and problem solving, of "positive constructive" daydreaming.

I've always been a big daydreamer, although I think I do my best creative thinking when I am alone and listening to music. Earth Wind and Fire's "Fantasy" has always been a great way for me to prime the pump.

Neil Gaiman, a prominent English author, offers his own formula for creativity. "For me, inspiration comes from a bunch of places: desperation, deadlines...A lot of times ideas will turn up when you're doing something else. And most of all, ideas come from confluence—they come from two things flowing together. They come, essentially, from daydreaming."[3]

Graham Wallas, a social psychologist and cofounder of the London School of Economics, offered a different angle: "We can often get more result in the same way by beginning several problems in succession, and voluntarily leaving them unfinished while we turn to others, than by finishing our work on each problem at one sitting."[4]

Cactus Jack Barringer, founder of Reality Sports Entertainment and inventor of a dozen successful products, had yet a different formula. "There's nothing like your subconscious for brainstorming. I identify a problem I think needs to be fixed, tell my mind to focus on it, and then I take a nap. I keep a pad by my bed and wake myself up and write down what comes to mind."[5]

—————— **❝** ——————

Creativity is a great motivator
because it makes people
interested in what they are doing.
Creativity gives hope that there can
be a worthwhile idea. Creativity
gives the possibility of some sort of
achievement to everyone.

– *Edward de Bono*

—————— **❞** ——————

If you want to create an innovative environment, you need to encourage your staff to daydream.

Consider or Throw Away (C.O.T.)

Another important thing to remember is that there are very few truly original ideas in this world. Creativity, according to Harvard psychologist Jerome Bruner,[6] is not the ability to generate a "new" idea but rather to take an old idea and apply it in a different context.

We've all heard stories about the trial and error process of famous inventors. One of my favorites is Thomas Edison's "invention" of a lighting system using circuits wired in parallel and bulbs with high-resistance filaments. At the time, scientific experts viewed the two things as incompatible, but Edison figured out how to make them work together.[7] After nine thousand experiments, the light bulb as we know it was born.

My experience certainly bears this out. The HBO promotion—the idea that made my career—was based on no-longer-innovative satellite technology, combined with a promotional sales format that Heritage had been using for years on its local channels. All I did was connect some dots in a new way.

But connecting the dots usually requires a lot of dots, so you want to encourage your staff to contribute their ideas. You want to make sure that they don't get discouraged because they feel their suggestions are carelessly dismissed or discarded. One approach to collecting those dots lies in three letters you've already seen: C.O.T. I initially viewed C.O.T. as a solution to the problem of stressed-out employees who misread my "creative" ideas as orders to be followed or tasks to be completed. What I wasn't expecting from C.O.T. was the breadth and depth of creativity that came as staff—from entry level to senior management—began to share their ideas more often, more openly, and more widely.

Many organizations offer the "opportunity" to submit ideas through the company suggestion box, but few staff find it an appealing option. Too often management reacts negatively when an employee doesn't understand all the implications of a suggestion. As bad, if not worse, is when management doesn't respond and is criticized for "not listening."

The C.O.T. method allows staff to share ideas with whichever coworkers might be interested, knowing that no one is expected to react positively or negatively at the moment. It also enlarges the pool of ideas that are available to be "connected" when the time is right.

Making Meetings Work

In the business world, we call group daydreaming "brainstorming."

Here are some tricks I've found to make meetings as creative as possible and make brainstorming work for you. Some may strike you as pretty obvious. Others, not so much.

Small Groups

The first time I learned the power of small groups was as a kid hanging out with a couple of the local farmers in the grain elevator on a rainy day. They sat around drinking soda pop and coffee and telling stories. As the hours passed, the stories just kept getting bigger and better.

Over the course of my career, I became more and more convinced that small groups are the start of assimilating and integrating new ideas.

In my experience, a group of two to eight people, preferably with a mix of backgrounds, comes close to the ideal size.

If you have fourteen people, divide them into two groups of seven. The more groups, the better.

And the more diversity the better.

Physical Setup

There's a reason why you keep hearing the phrase "a round table discussion."

When the boss sits at the head of the table and asks for ideas, s/he is the focus of the discussion. Participants glance at him/her for reactions and encouragement.

Brainstorming is most effective when the playing field is level and the participants all operate as equals. Sitting in the round is not a guarantee, but it sure does improve the odds.

Focus on the Problem

The more clearly you define the problem, the more focused the ideas will be.

One of my tasks at the lottery was to increase revenue. Gosh, I knew in the first minutes that it was much too broad a topic for anyone outside of the executive management team to have an opinion.

To break the challenge into manageable pieces, I asked staff to find ways to improve ticket distribution. After several discussions, we approved a suggestion to ship tickets directly to the retail stores by UPS, rather than having our sales reps deliver them in person. Faster, consistent delivery allowed the lottery to air commercials earlier; as a result, we increased sales by over $15 million. And by the way, the sales reps were freed up to work with the individual stores on what they thought they needed and wanted. That increased sales as well. Another challenge I lobbed out was to develop some new lottery games. One genuinely novel idea came from Larry Loss, the deputy director and a twenty-nine-year employee, who suggested a $20 game book. At first, the "Nomans" came out in force. The old-timers "knew" that no one would buy a $20 ticket in Iowa. The finance folks worried about the cost of changing lottery procedures (e.g., retail locations needed new dispensers, the prize payout system had to be adjusted). When we finally decided to take the risk, we ordered two years' worth of tickets. They sold out in four months!

Build Off Ideas

Brainstorming sessions can take a lesson from the rules of theatrical improvisation. Check out the websites for *Second City* in Chicago or *Saturday Night Live*.

Rule #1. Always agree to what your partner proposes. In real life, of course, people don't always agree, but any idea, no matter how ridiculous, might be the first step in developing a genuinely creative solution.

Rule #2. Always say "YES, AND..." Whatever idea is proposed, add something to it, expand on it, take it in a different direction. The first example of an adult after-hours event for the zoo simply wasn't workable, but several iterations later, we arrived at the incredibly successful Zoo Brew.

Another example was the exotic red bats. The original idea came from the owner of the Jefferson Telephone Company, who had a small exotic animal farm south of town. For years he'd done a Halloween display on bats at his farm, which was the spark that started the idea of the April Fools' Day parade. As our zoo staff looked for fun ways to improve upon his idea, someone came up with attaching two baseballs on one of the bats (to tell which bat was the male). Another staffer suggested we could tell the press that the bats came from Louisville (Louisville slugger, get it?) and needed "special" gloves to handle them (baseball gloves).

Rule #3. Make a statement rather than asking a question. Don't ask "how would you do that?" Instead, say, "Maybe we could do it [this way]." In other words, be a part of the solution.

Underlying the rules of improv is the notion that it takes a while to get the creative juices flowing. Research suggests that the first ideas to be voiced are those that are relatively familiar and closest to the surface of the mind. By building on each idea as it comes along, you stimulate others to explore ideas that are less obvious or less conventional.

An act that produces effective surprise is the hallmark of the creative enterprise. ... All of the forms of effective surprise grow out of a combinatorial activity—a placing of things in new perspectives.

— *Jerome Bruner*

An image I always liked, compliments of the management consultants Tom and David Kelley, is that creativity is like a muscle.[8] As I learned under Connolly and at Heritage, the more you use it, the stronger and more effective it gets.

There are a number of ways to get that creative muscle working. For example, you can ask everyone to come to the meeting with at least one or two ideas on a post-it note that can be put up on the wall as they enter. Be sure to ask for the ideas at the beginning of the meeting, so staff knows you are serious.

Another approach is to have the team work on a warm-up exercise. For example, you could ask each person to come with forty different ways to use a brick, a coin, or a rubber tire.

Another approach, which can be applied once a discussion has started, comes from Alex Osborn, the father of brainstorming, and later arranged by Bob Eberle into the mnemonic SCAMPER.

S = Substitute?

C = Combine?

A = Adapt?

M = Magnify? = Modify?

P = Put to other uses?

E = Eliminate?

R = Rearrange? = Reverse?

Whatever the topic, you apply the checklist of SCAMPER questions. You'll find that ideas start popping up almost involuntarily.

Yet another is to challenge your assumptions...all the things you think you know about the current situation.

List the assumptions (e.g., nobody will buy a Powerball ticket that costs more than $1).

Write down the opposite of each assumption (e.g., players have been buying scratch tickets at $5 and $10 for years).

Ask each participant to identify a way to accomplish each reversal.

The discussion about increasing the Powerball price from $1 to $2 felt like World War III, and it would never have happened if we hadn't worked through each of the assumptions. But it eventually got done and added several million dollars to Iowa's profits and over a billion to national lottery profits while providing a new and improved game for our customers.

Be Positive

Remembering the way my father, Charles Connolly, and Bill Riley always encouraged others, I consciously work to smile or nod positively when a staff member presents an idea. Looking deep in thought may suggest that you're smart, but it makes the idea-giver feel foolish.

Many times, of course, I really do like the idea. Sometimes I'm underwhelmed. Calculated or not, a smile is an unbeatable way to prime the pump.

Employees want to please the boss. Sometimes you don't know whether it's because they want your positive approval or they don't want to be fired or criticized. Whatever the motivation, you can't go wrong if you're really interested in their ideas—or if you compliment them when they try something different, whether or not it succeeds.

When you're trying to do this in a meeting context, there are some obvious tricks:

Be proactive in asking participants for suggestions. Let people know that you plan to call on everyone, and then do just that.

Don't ignore the quiet members, as they may have some of the best ideas.

Don't let anyone demur. Be patient and encouraging…provide space and time for each participant to formulate his or her ideas.

Applaud someone who speaks up for the first time.

Make a point of thanking someone who comes up with the really great idea, but do it one-on-one, after the meeting.

Save Judgments for Later

In an effective brainstorming session, there are *no bad* ideas. Every idea, no matter how small or outrageous, can plant a seed for a truly great idea. This is not the time to be evaluating the merits of the ideas. Just let the ideas flow.

In my experience, the greater the individual's expertise in a given area, the harder it is for that person to be enthusiastic about new ideas and approaches. That's hardly surprising—expertise is what makes the organization efficient and effective at what it's doing. But it is an obstacle to developing new ideas and approaches, a sure-fire way to miss opportunities to do it better.

—————— **"** ——————

It's better to have tried and failed than to succeed at doing nothing at all.

– *Charles Connolly*

—————— **"** ——————

It's even worse in a government operation like the lottery, where one mistake can cost millions of dollars. At our multistate lottery meetings, I watched in awe as some of my counterparts voted no on every issue. Their reason? "If I vote no and the project fails, I can say I was right on the issue. If I vote no and the project is successful, I can tell my governor that I had some reservations but am glad it worked."

So how do you eliminate the "Nomans"? One trick I've learned is to designate someone to watch for the negative signs—rolling eyes, sighs, shaking of heads, tapping of pencils—and point them out when they occur, perhaps using a buzzer or a beeper. Or impose a fine—perhaps a quarter or a dollar—on everyone who makes a negative comment or dismissive gesture.

By forewarning group members that these actions make a negative impression, you'll help to keep the ideas flowing.

Write Down Every Word

Designate a recorder and put ideas up on easel-size post-its where everyone can see them. By seeing all ideas, everyone has the opportunity to build on every idea.

And we all know, of course, that if you don't write it down, you'll forget it. So write down your own ideas, and when you don't have paper, send yourself an e-mail or a text.

Have Fun

Brainstorming should create supportive laughs, "yes" smiles, and a comfortable setting. Let your mind go...

I often give "warm-up" exercises that are unrelated to work so participants can get in the groove. One such exercise is to suggest a party with a scavenger hunt. Guests will be divided into five groups, each with a cell phone to record video tasks. Staff are asked to come up with ten ideas for skits to be produced and recorded in a two-hour period. I give an example like "the men have Mc-Donald's hats on with French fries sticking out of each ear singing 'Yankee Doodle Dandy.'"

"

Every time a man puts a new idea across, he faces a dozen men who thought of it before he did. But they only thought of it.

— *Oren Arnold*

"

A more dramatic approach is used by Bluespace Creative, a strategic marketing and design firm in Denison, Iowa. The creative "center" is a bright orange "playground for the mind,"[9] a decal-covered room with a carnival-like atmosphere, guarded by a monster moose head sporting an Elvis wig and sunglasses. When the search for inspiration is on, staff pile onto red beanbag cushions and don their thinking caps—perhaps a Viking helmet, a bomber hat with goggles, or a top hat. They start by making music. Sometimes they sing along to karaoke, and at other times they just make up stuff, using kazoos, bongos, or drumsticks.

Another option, if you don't want to be quite so silly, is to think about mixing sensory reactions. Questions suggested by the Kelleys might be:

- What word would taste like tomato soup?
- What would the word government taste like?
- What flavor best represents your attitude toward life?
- What occupation would taste like ear wax?
- What does a brainstorming session taste like?

As a last suggestion, keep brainstorming sessions short—no more than fifteen minutes to keep it fun and the ideas fresh.

Dare to Act

H. G. Wells said, "Human history is, in essence, a history of ideas. Everyone has them. Few know how to use them."

In my days at Heritage, I was reminded of several stunning examples of Wells's dictum.

In 1862, a German scientist named Phillip Reis demonstrated a mechanical device that could transmit music through a wire, but he had no luck in getting support for its commercial development. The experts he approached felt that there was no market for this "Telephon,"[10] as the telegraph provided adequate communication technology. Ten years later, Alexander Graham Bell patented the telephone.

A similar thing happened in 1968, when Spencer Silver, a chemist at 3M, developed an adhesive that could easily be lifted

---- **"** ----

In a moment of decision, the
best thing you can do is the right
thing, the next best thing is the
wrong thing, and the worst thing
you can do is nothing.

— *Theodore Roosevelt*

---- **"** ----

off, but no one at 3M saw any potential in it. Some years later, another 3M employee, Arthur Fry, grew tired of losing the page markers in his hymnal. When he coated them with Silver's adhesive, they stayed in place, but could be lifted off without damaging the page. This time 3M paid attention, but it was not until 1980 that Post-it Notes were born.

Here with some suggestions to improve the odds that your creative ideas become innovative solutions.

Allow Authority / Empower People

How many times have you been in a meeting in which one person has a good idea that everyone likes…and then someone else (with less passion for the idea) is given the authority to manage the project?

If it's your idea, it has a much greater chance of success if you're allowed to pursue it. I've seen it happen repeatedly throughout my career.

At Heritage, I was charged with getting the HBO folks on board with the idea of a movie promotion with a satellite uplink.

Everybody at Heritage thought the idea sounded good, but there was no one else who could make the case for a proposal that was still only half baked. By the time I'd worked through the chain of rejections at HBO, I knew exactly what we needed to do.

And perhaps, in the realm of putting my money where my mouth is, I've let Teri Wood, the lottery's VP of marketing, run her own show. I love marketing, and it would be so easy to end up micromanaging her. But I have great confidence in her leadership and try to stay out of her hair.

Provide Resources

A pretty logical idea, huh? Projects fail without the proper money, people, and time. When you have the right idea, make sure you are prepared and know how much of each you'll need.

That was a lesson I learned big-time at Heritage. I had the idea for the national HBO promotions, but the success of our initial telethon was due in large part to the direct mail blast prepared by the marketing department. If Jim Cownie had refused to fund it, my career would have looked very different.

The zoo had the same issues, except on a smaller scale. A couple of staff suggested that we let visitors feed crackers to the giraffes, a feature that was popular at a number of other zoos. At that point in my tenure, $5,000 to rebuild the display and provide platforms where visitors could reach the animals seemed like a big ask. But the idea was appealing, and we found the money. We recouped that money in less than a year, and the giraffes continue to be a big draw and to provide additional funding for animal care.

Be Nimble

Being nimble means embracing and encouraging change. Most of you have seen the entrepreneurial chart of start-up, innovation, and maturity.

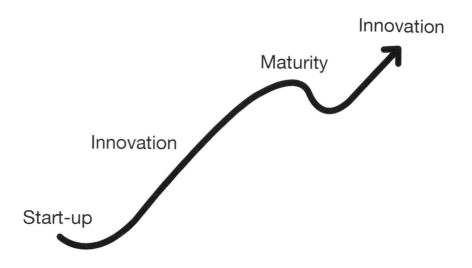

"Creating an innovative environment" – Terry Rich

Suppose you like banana ice cream, so you start up your own store and brand. There are hundreds like you who like banana ice cream, so with proper marketing and operations, you do pretty well for the first months. But now you've sold the ice cream to the "early adopters" and must find some other way to grow. Without innovating again, you will hit the maturity part of this graph and stagnate. Only by adding a new flavor or product through innovation will you continue to be truly successful.

In the real world, the example of the cable industry is near and dear to my heart. I spent a lot of years rubbing shoulders with executives of broadcast TV stations who couldn't imagine why anyone would pay for television. Heck, weren't four channels enough?

Jim Hoak, a cofounder of Heritage, was very nimble. He saw the potential for cable long before the days of satellite retransmission and long before there was any unique programming available for cable channels. For several years, he invested in what seemed like a losing proposition. I'll never forget the day in the mid-1970s when he predicted that we'd have programming via satellite within a year. Even at Heritage, the management team was skeptical, but within six months, we were pulling HBO movies from their satellites and retransmitting them nationwide. Hoak acted on his dream and had the infrastructure in place when the cable industry took off.

Another example is our not-always-beloved US Postal Service, which owned the communications world for many years at only four cents. But they rested on their laurels for far too long. Can you imagine the laughs at the executive meetings when they heard that FedEx would guarantee overnight, on-time delivery? Or the utter disbelief at the notion of sending e-mails or texts with immediate delivery and at minimal cost to the user?

A third example is Eastman Kodak, a company that *Economist* magazine called the Google of its day. According to *Forbes*, "Kodak did not fail because it missed the digital age. It actually invented the first digital camera in 1975. However, instead of marketing the new technology, the company held back for fear of hurting its lucrative film business, even after digital products were reshaping the market." I guess they thought we'd all be printing pictures rather than using Facebook.

Make a Decision

Accountants, lawyers, and IT personnel are paid to challenge every new idea and look for solutions that minimize risk. CEOs are paid to make decisions based on the balance of risk and reward in situations in which the outcome is rarely 100 percent assured.

I suspect that most CEOs walk into their offices most days scared of this responsibility. But all the successful entrepreneurs and CEOs I've met put on a confident face and make a decision to move on. Employees follow confidence. They will respond when you say "let's go." Until then, debate and indecision will prevail.

One of those make-or-break decisions for me came with a new lottery scheme—the Big Beeping Deal. When the machine "beeped" (for every twentieth ticket), the lottery would award $20 to the player. The promotion was so successful that we decided to extend the offer for another week. Except when the extended promotion began, the machine didn't beep. Our customers would never have known, but we announced it as soon as we found out and agreed to refund every ticket issued during that initial period. It cost us some money, but it bought a lot of loyalty from both lottery customers and staff.

Set Milestones

It can be very helpful to set milestones for any project you take on so as to identify individual goals, each of which seems manageable. It's also a way for management to monitor progress and identify unexpected problems before they sink the project.

The book *One Thing* notes that NASA was only on course 2 percent of the time when sending a spacecraft to the moon. By tracking the course in real time, they were able to make the proper corrections to land on the moon.

But the idea of milestones works both ways. Employees need to know how the overall organization is doing and how their contribution fits into the larger goals. Heritage management, from the beginning, sent all employees the monthly financials. I followed that trend at the zoo and at the lottery.

Be Willing to Fail

After my speeches, I always ask for feedback from my audience. One of the most common questions is "Haven't you ever had a failure? Your experiences seem too good to be true."

"

Failure is the tuition you pay for success.

– Walter Brunell

"

In fact, it's quite the opposite. I've had quite a few failures, starting with my humiliating defeat when I ran for president of the ISU student government. I have tried to see every failure as a learning experience. In that case, the lesson was that if it's worth doing, it's worth putting my best effort into it.

A more costly failure came during the RHI years, when I tried to develop a cable franchise for the NAIA College Baseball World Series. ESPN had a successful franchise with the NCAA College World Series in nearby Omaha. Why couldn't I do that with the NAIA?

Grand View University, the local host for the series, gave RHI a three-year option on the TV broadcast rights. When the Fox Sports Network agreed to carry the three games in return for half the ad revenue, I figured this would be a lay-up.

I booked the TV crew, a production truck, and a satellite up-link. Only then did I think to hire someone to sell the ads. I got a bad feeling in the pit of my stomach when he said with a shrug, "Well, it's a first-time event in Des Moines…and your lead time is too short to fit into the current year's budget."

It got worse when the stadium's management refused to let us park the TV truck on their new sod because of the heavy rain.

You guessed it. I lost $25,000 on three nicely produced but undersold televised games. Money that I could lose because I set funds aside to invest in new ideas. Failure on a project did not mean failure for my business.

———— **"** ————

You don't learn to walk by following rules. You learn by doing and by falling over.

— *Richard Branson*

———— **"** ————

One last thought comes from my favorite current philosopher, Brinley Dagestad, who taught me "Failure is the first step to success." Who's Brinley Dagestad? My granddaughter! You see, at age one and a half, she took her first step. What happened? She failed and fell down. The next day, she took another step and fell. Soon she succeeded in walking all over the house. But if she hadn't tried, rather than tried and failed, she would have been like many of you who have the million-dollar idea, but never put it into action.

And don't forget ... I failed to produce any interest in Cooper from forty-three of the forty-four letters I sent. But I'm sure glad I sent all forty-four.

"Yep, Happiness happens on the way to success."

Footnotes

1. Lewis M. Terman, "Genetic Studies of Genius."
2. Rebecca L. McMillan and Scott Barry Kaufman, "Ode to Positive Constructive Daydreaming," *Frontiers in Psychology*, September 2013.
3. Neil Gaiman, response during the Q&A after his December 2011 Wheeler Center interview.
4. Graham Wallas, *The Art of Thought*, 1926.
5. "The Innovation Toolkit," *Entrepreneur*, May 2003.
6. "The Conditions of Creativity," *On Knowing: Essays for the Left Hand*, Harvard University Press, 1979.
7. *Edison, His Life and Inventions,* Dyer, Frank L and Martin, Thomas C., Project Gutenberg, 2013
8. *Creative Confidence*, Tom Kelley and David Kelley, Crown Business, 2013.
9. Gottschalk, Mary, *Creative Work Room*, Iowan Magazine, July/August 2013.
10. *Bell 'did not invent telephone'*, http://news.bbc.co.uk/2/hi/science/nature/3253174.stm

About the Author

Terry Rich is a lifelong farm kid who has served in many national leadership roles, including president and CEO of the Iowa Lottery and president of the North American Association of State and Provincial Lotteries. Prior to that, he was CEO of the Blank Park Zoo and president and CEO of Rich Heritage Inc.

As an entrepreneur, Terry developed Rich Heritage Inc., along with four other companies, including radio station KBBM, US Digital Video, Newsletter Ease, and the World Championship Socker League LLC.

He has appeared on national television in many roles, including a lottery industry expert on ABC, NBC, CBS, and CNN, movie host on Starz!, and as a panel guest on *The Tonight Show*.

Raised on a farm near Cooper, Iowa, Terry has won numerous entrepreneurial and leadership awards in television production and marketing. He has a bachelor of science degree in speech from Iowa State University, is governor emeritus at ISU, and director emeritus of the Blank Park Zoo.

As CEO of the Iowa Lottery, Terry oversees Iowa's $300+-million-dollar lottery enterprise. He also serves as marketing chair on the board of Powerball.

Made in the USA
San Bernardino, CA
05 November 2015